D0882103

It's Not About You, It's About Your Message

How to Hook and Hold Any Audience

Katie Karlovitz

with Michael Bettencourt

For Himself, John Quinn

And to the memory of my brother Eric

ACKNOWLEDGEMENTS

Writing a book is a shockingly demanding process and affords a lot of time to think about everything else.

Thank you, with all my heart:

- Adele, Bela, Mark, Anne, Eric, Matthew & Betsy Karlovitz
- My extended family of Karlovitz & Mosleners, nieces & nephew, grandnieces and cousins all
- My fabulous in-laws and out-laws
- My fantastic friends: Janice & Ron, Lynka & Ron, Jeannie & Nick, Janet, Rose, Charlie, Paul, Eric & Gayle, Michael & Maria, Mary Shakun
- Book Club: Janet, Janet, Lynka, Roslyn, Lisa, Robin, Sharlene, Deanie Bird, & Giovanna
- My inspired teachers, mentors & coaches, most especially Alan Sklar, Teresa Marinelli and Justine Clay
- In Good Company in NYC: Victoria, Ad, Amy, Donna & all the smart ladies- Alice, Ann, Caroline, Cody, Diane, Emily, Evie, JB, Jenny, Justine, Linda, et al – could not have done it without you
- Best designer ever, Cody
- Running–With–Heels NYC, Jenny and our high-heeled gang: Susie, Veronica, Rhonda, Sheilah, Nicole, Alice and Lady Bug Garette
- Tylene & Ryan Levesque, & Lynn & Yassin Sahar, Selena Soo & the entire NLM posse
- My excellent doctors: Bruce Chung, Paul & Beth White, Lillian Mittl, Nancy Jacobs
- My gentle vet William Friedman
- My smart, sturdy editors: Becky, Emily, Julia and Aran

- My invaluable assistants, Emily & Havah
- The best Board of Advisors: Janet, Rose, Will, Teresa & Miriam
- My hair wrangler Chrystoph & dog wrangler Robert
- My precious four-footed family—Louis, Charlie, Riley & Teddy
- Mt. Lebanon High School, Michael, Mr. Meyers
- Carnegie Mellon University, the Drama Department, Lauren Henry
- New School University
- The International Rescue Committee
- The New York Women's Foundation
- Each and every one of my audio engineers
- Everyone I've ever worked with
- Mary Weekes
- Mikey O
- My dark knight, Michael Bettencourt
- And to President Obama, for always keeping it real and keeping it classy. Bravo.

Contents

Introduction

"Be yourself; everyone else is already taken!"
Oscar Wilde

From the Walk of Hell
to the Waldorf Astoria

The client I'm huddled backstage with, Isaac, was only seven when his village in the Sudan was burnt to the ground by violent terrorists called the Janjaweed.

He then spent the next seven years in hell with thousands of other boys—walking, always walking—to avoid being captured and killed.

Now, he's about to take center stage at the Waldorf Astoria Hotel in New York City, and his eyes are wide. Standing next to him in the wings, I'm hoping he can't sense how hard my heart is pounding. I've been coaching him for the last two days, and the stakes are unusually high.

If Isaac can connect with this silky sea of posh New Yorkers in the audience, they'll be moved to give more money and support to the group that helped rescue him, the International Rescue Committee. In this instance, it literally means more lives will be saved. It's an incredible amount of pressure on a young man who's only been in America for a couple of months.

* * *

I'd first spoken to Isaac four weeks previously—we'd been getting to know each other on the phone, after the IRC asked me to help him prepare for his speech.

Then he arrived in New York with forty-eight hours to go until the speech.

We didn't have a lot of time—either to write or rehearse, or for the delivery of the speech itself. Isaac would have just five minutes to get the job done, which was to move and inspire his audience.

We needed to simplify his story while keeping its heart-breaking power—*without* falling into sensationalism. If humanly possible, we had to end on a high note.

That would be challenging enough for an experienced public speaker, let alone someone who has never previously spoken in public, and whose first language isn't English.

* * *

We had five sessions together over the two days.

We focus intently on the essence of the story—on the terror he felt, on how he survived when so many other young boys died.

We need to make his story clear and easy to follow—to give the audience time to process this awful, alien scenario.

As we practice, his voice gets softer and his shoulders sag. Reliving this nightmare drains him, but he's determined to share his story and to help others. He somehow intuits how much help this will be to others, and he lets me guide him. We trust each other to come quickly to the truth at hand, and then find a way to put it into the appropriate words that he can voice comfortably.

We use up every minute we have to rehearse—I'll be showing you exactly how to do what Isaac did a little later on—and then it's time to head to the Waldorf.

It's all happened so quickly, it feels like we're being shot out of a story cannon and hurtling towards our audience. I can't imagine what Isaac's thinking, and I wonder if he's ever seen snow before. There's a gentle flurry of it as we hail a taxi.

* * *

We huddle together in the darkened theater wing.

I listen intently for the presenter to say Isaac's name, and realize that I'm holding my breath.

The introduction begins—there's his cue!—we hug quickly, and Isaac heads out into the light of the stage and crosses to the podium with a sure step.

He pauses and looks out at the audience—just as we'd rehearsed it—he breathes for a count of three, and then gently—slowly—begins to tell his story.

The room is intensely, deeply quiet.

He has them.

He remembers every note I gave him, and he absolutely nails his delivery.

Then it's over, and the audience are standing, clapping, crying—and Tom Brokaw, the host of the evening, returns to the stage in tears himself.

* * *

Such is the power and the gift of speaking in public.

And results like this are the norm—not the exception—if you follow the right steps.

Those steps are exactly what you're going to learn, story by story, example by example, in this book.

You're going to see how people get ready to on—how they prepare every bit as thoroughly as if they were actors getting ready to go onstage.

Every speech, every presentation, is a performance. It's more (much more) than just "being yourself" or "speaking from the heart."

You need to be ready for show time—you need to make careful choices about your content, shaping your message, practicing your delivery and even making sure that you've worn the right clothes and eaten the right food.

You're also going to learn how to work 'from the inside out'—how to make choices based on your own individual sense of what is natural and comfortable, and not on what other people are saying or doing.

You're going to see the specific challenges faced by some of the clients I've worked with, the choices they made, the goals they aimed for, and the results they achieved.

These skills are fairly simple to learn, and you can acquire them at any point in your lifetime.

You don't need a lot of money, time, or special equipment.

You can be any type, size, look, ethnicity, or age in order to master them.

In fact, just as you are now is perfect.

* * *

This book is for anyone who wants to speak more comfortably in public, either for business or personal purposes. It takes you step-by-step through the process of preparing to go "onstage." These techniques can accommodate any situation and message, and offer a clean, straightforward, and playful approach.

Don't take yourself too seriously, but do take your prep seriously.

Learning these basics will free you to create speeches, workshops, webinars, and podcasts that are compelling to listen to and hard for the audiences to forget.

What would you choose to speak about, if you could?

What are you enthusiastic and emotional about?

What message do you want to get across to more people?

If you can talk about it, you can share it.

Are you ready to transform yourself into a confident, engaging, and memorable speaker?

Then please turn the page.

Chapter 1: Making The Most of What You've Already Got

"Is not life a thousand times too short for us to bore ourselves?" Friedrich Nietzsche

What is it that makes some people such riveting speakers? Are they genetically encoded such that the rest of us just *have* to pay attention to them? And if yes, what about regular people? Or the ones who are introverts or shy?

While some people do have an innate talent for public speaking, their success does not depend on a magic alchemy but on something mundane and un-mysterious: good preparation. Anyone can learn the elements of preparing well for a public speaking event and introverts are more inclined to learn those lessons better that extroverts, who don't always feel that they need them.

Let's take a look at how my husband John became an accomplished speaker and what you can learn from his experience.

"We'd like you to give a speech."

When John called me, I knew from his tone that something was up. He'd just won a Service Excellence award from his employer, New School University, which included money and two Yankees tickets (which he loved), and *giving an acceptance speech* (which he loathed).

My husband comes from a large family, many of whom describe themselves as "shy," meaning "when I'm around new people or groups I will keep quiet, but in the family, I'm fine." I see this in my practice, where a cultural or family influence applies a pressure to keep quiet. (To address this, my intake questionnaire asks how you were treated growing up regarding expressing yourself.) I knew John's family history, and I knew that he'd never given a formal speech before, but I also knew that with the right preparation, he would be able to pull this off like a virtuoso.

His first impulse was to describe what he did at the job. However, when I asked him "If you were in the audience, would you be interested in this?" he saw my point. It might have seemed relevant, but it was boring. As an alternative, I suggested he tell a few entertaining job-related stories and, even more important for a university audience, tell them what going back to college in his early 50s to complete bachelor's and master's degrees meant to him. As an employee, he'd taken evening classes for several years, and it was an education for which he had worked hard.

He agreed with my suggestions, said he understood my advice, and had it under control. He was simultaneously finishing his master's thesis, so while I kept asking about his progress on the script, I wasn't actually seeing it. But he had enough of a jump on it, so I assumed he'd be fine.

He was not fine.

Thirty-six hours before he was to go onstage, John came into my office with such a stricken look on his face that I thought someone had died. He confessed that he'd only written a single paragraph of his speech.

We now had an official public speaking emergency.

Because we didn't have time to do a real collaboration, I took over the script-writing chore, which he handed over with great relief. Knowing him as I do, I wrote a version that allowed his innate humanity and humor to come out.

Together we fine-tuned the script to suit his natural speech patterns. The result was easy for him to deliver and genuinely inspiring. We rehearsed as much as we could in the short time we had. I told him not to try to memorize the script but, instead, familiarize himself with it, which he did by speaking it, timing it, tweaking the rhythms, and speaking it again.

We also printed it out on big cards in a large font. This script was going to be his prop, something he could use to keep him aligned with his message, so we needed to adjust the scale of it. When you're presenting live in front of an audience, it's easier to find your place quickly with a larger font size.

Even in this short amount of time, I could already see the transformation happen as he learned to play with his style, regulate his pacing, and ease into owning his message. Still, when we went to bed that night, I prayed to the gods of public speaking to stay with him.

He got up early, and ate a light breakfast of fruit, granola and tea (instead of coffee), and told me where to meet him on campus. He was getting there an hour early to settle into the space and get used to its look and energy. And off he went.

The ceremony began at 10 am. The room was packed, with a camera crew, a sound engineer, a still photographer, the brand new president of The New School University, family, friends, staff, and five *extremely* somber-looking awardees.

I could sense John's electricity when he put his hand on my back to steer me to my seat. He was going to speak first, which I was glad to hear, because being first out of the gate meant he wouldn't lose energy in nervous waiting.

The lights dimmed and the ceremony began with the requisite boring PowerPoint presentation. Then John was at the podium. He took a slight pause (as we'd rehearsed, as Isaac had, as everyone should) and began.

His breathing was under his control, he was mentally present, and he connected to the audience as he told his story. Feeling his oats, he even threw in some ad libs, got a number of laughs, and twice had to stop mid-sentence for applause. Not bad at all, and definitely not shy.

The preparation we had done enabled John to combine his personality with his distinctive view of the university to craft an engaging and personalized "thank you" for his award.

My husband also learned what all my speakers have learned when they've gone through this process: We all have a stage-worthy story or idea or question to offer to the world;

the challenge is to figure out what that is and then transform yourself into a public speaker to deliver it.

How to Prepare Your Own Speech

Selecting and Refining the Topic

Here's how to get ready for showtime, whether your topic has been assigned to you or you have the freedom to choose what you want to talk about.

Begin by collecting all manner of things that are in any way related to your general topic, the operative word here being *general*.

- articles and quotes you've saved
- video clips you like
- interviews with authorities you admire
- audio content
- music tracks
- poetry and images

Don't restrict your gathering at this stage because it's too soon to know what will or won't work. Just pull in everything that might aid you in getting your point across.

Once you have gathered a nice juicy cache of content, start separating the wheat from the chaff. Pick a time that's ideal for you to let your brain out to play. Put on your favorite "music to think by" and turn off your other devices. You want to spread all your goodies out in front of you so that you can see them and they can see you. (I do this in my dining room, where I can, literally, put everything on the table.)

Take a few deep breaths, try not to think too hard, and just notice your thoughts about what you're looking at, and then your feelings, a fertile and lively cross-stream of intellect and emotion. Rather than dispatching your brain to make decisions, allow your choices to come to you on their own.

More Questions to Ask—Audience Analysis:

- What time of day is my event?
- What is the space (also called "venue") like?
- Approximately how many people are expected?
- What is the age range and what is the average age?
- How do they breakdown by gender?
- What is the ethnic composition?
- What do they already know about my topic?
- Are they attending by choice?
- What do they most urgently need from me?
- What can I find out about them, beforehand?

The **time of day** is significant because of human physiology. With a mid-morning event, most of your audience will be alert. A few hours later—say, 12:30—then hunger becomes a factor. Around 4:00, then low-blood sugar is a factor. After dinner, digestion and wine come into play.

The space will have its own energy and feel, and, if you have the chance, try to visit it so that you'll have an idea of what you're walking into. Knowing the venue in advance means that you will lose little energy making adjustments to the space, which gives you more energy to maintain a focus on your message. Always ask for photos to be sent to you if you haven't been in the venue before.

The **number of people** you'll be addressing will affect your delivery. With more than thirty to forty people in the room, use a microphone. Human bodies, upholstery, carpeting, and curtains are "sound soaks," and if you're in such a space, you'll need extra projection of your voice to keep an intimacy with the audience, whatever its size.

When speaking, be mindful of the **generations, genders, and ethnicities** in the seats. Sensitivity to the interplay of these differences will inform your choice of vocabulary and content.

If you have a way to pre-gauge your audience's **level of knowledge** on your topic, all the better. If you don't, then assume they have a generalist's knowledge and aim for just about their heads, intellectually speaking. Let them reach up rather than you talking down.

For an audience **compelled to attend,** clearly demonstrate your good will and expertise (and sympathy) in the first twenty seconds of your opening. When they are hooked and eager to listen to you, they will savor your every word, breath, and sigh. Give them whatever you can to make it **worth their time and attention,** and ask yourself how you can help *right now,* as well as later.

Building the Launch

The simplest way to shape your comments and structure your ideas is the most time-honored: beginning, middle, and end.

The beginning is the most crucial of the three parts. Be inventive, be unpredictable, be yourself, and I guarantee you, it will pay off.

- Instead of the standard "Good afternoon ladies and gentleman, and thank you all for taking time out of your busy day to be with me," try something like "On the first day of my first job, I learned the most important tip I've ever been given, and I'm here today because you need to know it, too."

- Rather than "It's an honor to be here today," why not say, "Getting to be with you now just thrills me and here's why..."

- Instead of "We're really excited to share this cutting-edge technology with you" try "You're about to experience something that will blow your mind and take your breath away." (I know that clichés are a no-no, but sometimes you have to use them; just use discretion.)

- "Hello, good morning and welcome to our program, everybody" could be replaced with "On my way here this morning, I saw the strangest thing ever, and here's what happened..."

From a theatrical point of view, you're hooking the audience's interest and curiosity by demonstrating fresh thinking at the top instead of opening with the same old lines that everyone uses and holding back the stronger, more original content for later. (In fact, there may not be a "later" since they've already tuned you out.)

The middle has to bring the audience along a path that goes from point A to B to C. The path may be straight or it might meander – either is fine as long as you understand where you're going with your message. If you know, then the audience will. If you don't, then they'll know that you don't.

Use muscular words whenever possible: descriptive and apt choices give wings to your ideas and traction to your reasoning. As Mark Twain said, "The difference between the right word and the almost right word is the difference between lightning and a lightning bug."

Never give a disclaimer in a speech, for any reason. Ever. Examples include "I hope I won't bore you," "I'll try to be as quick as possible," "Just getting over a cold, so hopefully everyone can hear me," and so on. It makes you look apologetic before you've even begun, and you're unwittingly telling the audience to find fault.

Avoid phrases such as "to be honest with you" and "to tell you the truth," which suggest that the speaker isn't normally truthful but that this audience is so special that the speaker will be honest.

Your ending should have a "take away" that leaves everyone with something to think about. It's the second most important of the three parts of your structure because this is what will be ringing in their ears after you finish.

Here are some suggestions:

- A call to action, something that you'd like them to do now: sign up for a mailing list, leave a business card, take one of these cards for a discount, and so on
- An inspirational quote, story, video clip, photo, or music that ends on a high note

- A challenge to do something unusual, important, or slightly outrageous/out of character/out of the comfort zone

By going through these steps, you're learning how to own your message, and once you own your message, you can trust yourself to be interesting.

Going through this deliberative process helps you start crafting your message by working only with those thoughts, questions, and ideas that matter to you. Start to select some of the things and play around with them. How well do they work together? How does this quote support my opening point? If I start with this, what should come next? Move things around, play with the order, and have fun with your puzzle pieces. Take the best of the best and return the rest to the folder for your future events.

At this point, you haven't boxed yourself in by writing what you think you should say or what you're expected to say. Instead, you accessed yourself on a deeper level, which will make it easier for you to be true to yourself and trust your gut.

Try to keep this an organic and fluid process, and not a battle of wits in your brain, even if, especially if, this process of preparation is being made at a time of great stress and pressure. Every single thing you decide to keep must be personal to you, but it must also have a good strategic reason for making the cut. If you can't justify it beyond "I'd like to use it," that's not quite good enough because everything you pick must further the audience's understanding of your message.

There's only one thing that can get between you and your inner performer: fear. We'll talk about that next.

Key points from Chapter 1:

- Skillful speakers know that they can't tell their audience everything, so they choose their material based on audience analysis and asking the right questions.

- Just because you've never given a good speech before doesn't mean you can't do it now. You can.

- Family or cultural pressure not to speak up must be addressed and resolved, in order to empower the speaker.

- Don't wait until the last minute to write your script.

- Practice by reading out loud and timing yourself...your running times should be consistent.

- Always eat a light breakfast on the day of your speech.

- Arrive at your venue early, and if possible, get photos of it well in advance.

- If possible, request going early in the speaker line-up.

Chapter 2: "Feel The Fear and Do It Anyway"

"There are two kinds of speakers: those that are nervous and those that are liars."
Mark Twain

Introduction

In the United States, the status of public speaking has declined in the last 50 years. In previous centuries, orations and speech-making were fashionable platforms for citizen interaction. Gatherings for popular orators such as Mark Twain and Oscar Wilde were well-attended social events, lasting for hours, with regular breaks for refreshment and sidebars.

And let's not forget the great sermon-makers, from Jonathan Edwards all the way through to Billy Graham, who inspired and moved people. Where did those traditions go?

I researched numerous images of report cards from the turn of the last century forward, and it became clear how much emphasis *used* to be placed on being well spoken and articulate. Not that long ago, speech-making was deemed an essential part of an American education and of being an American citizen.

But at some point after the mid-twentieth century, public speaking was dropped from school curricula and ceased to be a requirement. From what I can deduce, it was around the late 1960s and early 1970s that report cards no longer showed it as a required course. By 1977, *The Book of Lists* put "Fear of Public Speaking" in its # 1 spot, ahead of the fear of death. Jerry Seinfeld had a field day with it in one of his acts, and a quick Google search shows that its ranking hasn't budged in over *three decades*.

Because of this lack of familiarity with public speaking, many people have now become afraid of speaking out and behave accordingly:

- Contributing little or nothing in meetings
- Never volunteering to organize and promote company programs
- Staying in the background during social business events
- Sending an email instead of picking up the phone
- Avoiding applying for certain jobs/careers because it involves speaking in public

The fear, however, comes from a lack of information about what is involved in the process of preparing for public speaking. The best possible remedy is to replace the fear with knowledge, since info is ammo. Once you learn how to prep for any public appearance, you can learn how to harness the fear in order to achieve your presenting goals.

This takes two steps: unlinking the fear from its source (which usually has something to do with shame and embarrassment) and then "burning" it.

Let's learn how to do this from Derek.

The Power of Childhood

Derek is a perfect example of someone who claimed a fresh voice for himself by shedding his fear.

The household he grew up in discouraged all conversation, expressions of opinions, or the asking of questions. Only the father spoke freely in the family of six, and when he did, he berated his wife and diminished his children. Their mother had long ago given up, and Derek and his brothers were bullied into keeping quiet because their survival depended on it.

As a result, Derek chose a profession that always puts him behind the scenes of the main action. He's well liked and intelligent, but when it comes to speaking his mind, when all eyes are on him, he "gets stuck," as he puts it. He expresses this through modifiers that both diminish him and allow him to hide: "It's *kind of* an honor" or "I'm glad they *sort of seem* to like me." This habit of self-shrinking his opinions frustrated him.

Being behind the scenes, however, didn't mean that he went unnoticed, and when he got a call telling him he'd been given an award for his excellent work and would have to give a speech, he wasn't sure if he was happy or horrified. (Does this sound familiar?) We began our coaching.

When working with someone like Derek, who needed to overcome a lifetime of holding his tongue, the first challenge, and the biggest, is to help them see that their voices and thoughts have value, to audiences and to themselves. When we speak our truths out loud, they take on a different energy than when we keep them to ourselves, and that difference is an empowering one.

Clearing that hurdle, then, makes it easier to come up with something to say that's a good fit for the speaker and the event. The award Derek was receiving was in memory of someone, so I asked him what he knew about the man for whom it's named. This struck him as a good place to start gathering information, and after some research, including speaking with the man's son, Derek said, "I wish I had met the man—everyone's telling me how inspiring he was." To which I replied, "And *that's* the beginning of your speech."

The script we came up with was original, moving, and, most importantly, comfortable for Derek to deliver. We then moved into the rehearsal phase (much of which we did over Skype, which served us well). We worked through the script slowly, seeking that balance between telling the audience what they needed to know about the man's essence while letting them use their imaginations to comprehend the man's legacy. The focus was always on that and not on Derek.

The speech we created was in striking contrast to Derek's behavior just six weeks earlier. During our time together, he had shifted his emotional energy, and now he had a new calm about him. I wasn't in the audience when he gave his speech, but I did see it later, on Facebook. He gave an astonishing performance.

I could see the emotional baggage around feeling tongue-tied just fall away. He was at ease and in control of himself. He got some laughs and knew to hold for them, and the audience appreciated what he was saying. You could feel the love. He has never been stuck since.

Unlinking and Burning

Step 1: Unlink It

"All is energy." Albert Einstein

The first step is to come to terms with any shame or embarrassment in your past that keeps you stuck in your fear of speaking. For me, it was Miss Kiefer's first-grade assembly, when I got caught in front of the red velvet curtain after it closed and everyone laughed as I tried to make it into the wings. Oh, the horrible, merry laughter in the audience!

One client was finally able to trace her dread and stage panic all the way back to a speech she gave in Paris forty years ago. Someone in the audience interrupted her, and she'd felt helpless to protect herself. She'd blanked out the memory, but her body had never forgotten the trauma. Subconsciously, she was linking the moment in Paris to giving speeches in general, so it's no wonder she felt dread.

Here are the steps to take to extricate yourself from the grip of your malevolent memories.

First, it's imperative to empty out *all* negative thoughts and beliefs associated with public speaking, performing, and even existing. The wisdom of the Chinese in the *I Ching* (*The Book of Changes*) advises "emptying your ting," which literally means "cauldron," in order to have the free space to receive whatever it is you seek. That's why we have to be scrupulous about getting rid of the junk first. I want you to recall and root out all the bad feelings, memories, and upsetting images that are hiding out in your body and soul.

Keeping a journal for this part of your speaker training will help you track all of the psychic sludge that will inevitably start to bubble up in your consciousness. Here's a starter list of memories you can delete from your brain's hard drive, and feel free to add to the list.

- Any and all performance mishaps: speaking in public, sporting events and games, music recitals, flubbing a punch line in a joke, social disasters
- Disparaging, negative talk you've heard about public speaking, as well as horror stories that others insist on sharing with you
- All negative, unhealthy comparisons of yourself to other people
- Family influences to keep quiet
- Cultural pressure to conform
- Anything else standing between you and your freedom of speech

Again, don't underestimate the potential harm based on a memory's age or seeming triviality. ("That was years ago, I'm fine!") Tally up as much as you can, noting the details but without judgment or attachment. Be specific, especially tuning in to how you were feeling. *That's* where the emotional charge is still sticking in you and where you're most tender and vulnerable.

Look everything over and see where details and associations might be coming back to bite you. Write them down, the grimier the better, and then take a moment to sit with them, not to deny or reject them, but just *to be* with them.

Look at your list, and as you do, completely detach yourself from the words on the page. Observe yourself coolly and firmly severing that tired, old energetic tie from them to you.

Now note the flimsiness of an old memory when you no longer have a personal connection to it. It's just a hollow little shell with nothing living in it anymore. Its powers are drained, along with your desire to retain them.

Step 2: Burn It

I urge you to have fun with this next step, which is to destroy what's left behind. Burn up your papers and blow away the ashes; shred them into confetti; rip them up and flush them away—whatever works for you. Then, as you clear out the physical remnants of the past, consciously release the wounds, the bruised feelings, and the anxiety that the words had for you.

Bye bye bad memories.

One inventive client twisted up her pages and used them to light the barbecue, and then made delicious pulled pork sandwiches for her family!

Allow yourself to savor the freedom of being completely emptied out of all the gunk and grime of the past. Your ting is empty, and your chance to transform into an inspired speaker is waiting for you.

Key points from Chapter 2:

- Historically, Americans did not fear public speaking.

- Just because you don't remember a trauma doesn't mean that it's forgotten about you.
- Re-playing the negative event keeps it alive and real for you. Combat it by unlinking it, then burning it.
- Everything is energy, including fear and its opposite, courage.
- You, and only you, have the power to manage your stage fright.
- It's all just energy.

Chapter 3: Confidence

"We are all worms, but I do believe that I am a glowworm." Winston Churchill

Introduction

Stephanie Zamora, in a HuffPost essay back in 2013, defined confidence as depending on "one *incredibly simple* thing" (italics original), which she called "owning it":

> When you're "owning it," it means that you're totally and completely at peace with who you are in every moment, interaction and experience…. You radiate charismatic energy whether or not you have an extroverted personality because you are genuinely content with yourself and your present experience.

So how do we get to this blessed state? How can we stop the inner monologue, find a mantra, and practice being comfortable with who we are?

Let's meet Asher and see how he owned himself.

Banking is actually incredibly interesting!

Asher was *brilliant* at divining the murk of the banking industry. Standard & Poor's, his employer, told him that he was going to represent the firm on a popular hyper-aggressive, fast-talking financial program on television. Not

"Would you?" but "You are going to be the public face of this highly respected Wall Street business." Accept it or resign. They made him an offer he couldn't refuse. He accepted.

Asher had already been on the show a few times and found the warp-speed analytical sound-bites and rapid cuts between anchor and guests unnerving. His lack of self-confidence began to gnaw at him, and I got the call.

We began with some respectful yet direct attention to Asher's self-doubts and unfavorable beliefs about himself. He'd decided that everyone else on the show was better than he, especially Darius, who had a cool command of the camera. Because he looked and sounded completely different from Asher, Asher had decided that he was therefore "less than" Darius.

Plus, his boss, the one who had put him on the show in the first place, didn't make the situation any better when she told him that he looked "wishy-washy" on camera.

To upgrade his professional pride, we studied video clips from the show. He saw himself as less flashy and more subdued than the other commentators. I agreed but pointed out that he had his own gravitas, and given that the topic was international banking, he came across as mature and better informed than his peers.

Feeling anxious and under pressure, it was easy for him to conclude that because he didn't come across the way Darius did, that his boss's assessment was right. It had been hard for him to see that, in fact, he had done a great many things well.

Asher and I ran drills. I lobbed questions at him the way the show host did, with the purpose of getting his brain connected with his lips in shorter and shorter intervals. I didn't want him to have time to think beyond the immediate answer. We rehearsed in person, over the phone, and with Skype.

After his fourth coaching session, we could both see the profound change in him. He now had a confident tone, comfortable with his own style and voice, because he had focused on the internal, the stuff he knew best (and precisely the reason he'd been put on the show in the first place.) He didn't try to be someone other than the someone he was: a soft-spoken conservative dresser and a careful thinker, smart and articulate on live TV.

In having a technique anchored in who Asher knew himself to be, and what he genuinely believed in, he learned how to own himself. Once he had that in play, he was then able to control his emotions.

It wasn't long before reporters at Bloomberg, MSNBC, and CNN started commenting on how good his pieces were, and within Wall Street, word got around. His boss backed off on the criticism and then promoted him.

The moral of the story: Confidence isn't located in an eye color, the cut of a suit, a haircut, watch, or a piece of jewelry. It comes from within, when speakers are comfortably connecting with their messages. Confident people are prepared and flexible, able to stay in the moment and not race to get ahead of themselves. That is called owning it, instead of it owning you.

How to Own It

Tuning in to the Inner Monologue

Our inner monologues never seem to take a break. We have a running commentary on our existence, 24/7. The percentage of negative or disparaging thoughts any one of us might have in a short time period can be shockingly high. We'd *never* tolerate someone else talking to us the way we talk to ourselves. "Research has shown that the majority of our self-talk is negative, therefore, is working against us rather than for us. These negative thoughts create...anger, irritation, frustration, hopelessness and disappointment" (Helmstetter, 1982; Stranulis & Manning, 2002, University of Lethbridge).

The fix for this is two-part. First, catch yourself having the negative thought in the moment you're having it (see Chapter 2, including "emptying your ting"). This can be tricky if you're so used to having toxic thoughts that you no longer notice having them. You can't adjust what you can't perceive, so tuning into your thoughts is the only way you'll be able to do that.

Find the Mantra

Once you do realize that you're focusing on upsetting outcomes, interrupt the thought at once and pop in its opposite. Tell yourself what you want to do (which is an action) instead of thinking about what you want to avoid (the less dynamic reaction.) Here some suggestions for you:

- I'm going to crush this!
- This is fun, and I am sweet.
- Fly high, land soft!
- I am sleek, smart, and strong.
- Time to blaze away!
- I've got this.
- And... we have lift-off!
- No limits ever.
- Blast it out of the park!

Now, you might have snickered at those motivational business posters, like the one with the mountain climber triumphantly conquering the summit with the words "Reach your peak!" But really, which is better? Saying to yourself, "I'm going to blow it" or latching onto more inspirational thoughts?

These short bursts of moral self-support and healthy psychic re-alignment are called mantras. Always use them in the present tense: "I am," not "One day I will be...." This makes their energy immediate and real rather than postponing its potency.

The psychology of using self-talk for a positive outcome is useful for keeping a productive frame of mind. The brain doesn't care which path we take, positive or negative. It's an equal-opportunity conveyor of thoughts. As Hamlet knows, "There is nothing either good or bad, but thinking makes it so."

As long as we have a choice in the matter of how to think (and if we don't control our thoughts, who does?), we should *always* choose in favor of ourselves.

Your mantra will be your personal, private antidote for the poisonous thoughts that haunt you. So rather than "I'm terrified of losing my train of thought," you tell yourself "I'm smart and focused." Instead of "What if no one pays attention?", you say, "I am prepared, engaging, and on topic." Whatever scares you, acknowledge it so you can control it.

The simple goal is to set your sights on what you want rather than on what you wish to avoid. It re-directs what could be a toxic thought into one that's healthy. It builds you up instead of tearing you down.

Practice Being Comfortable

You might create a vision board as you experiment with your style of communicating. Images convey information differently than words, and more quickly. Play with strong bold pictures and drawings. Experiment with color. Do certain shades and tones suggest particular feelings?

Another way to grow your confidence is meditating. It makes everything in life a bit calmer, and I think that that comfort lends itself well to any type of performing. Phil Jackson encourages his basketball players to meditate because of the positive results he sees in their play.

As you experiment with these tips, you'll notice that you'll start to feel more natural where you once felt self-conscious. The audience, in turn, will be able to hear you well, without anything (such as yourself) getting in the way. It's win/win for all, allowing for a deeper connection among speaker, message, and audience.

Key Points from Chapter 3:

- Confidence is not located in one place in the body, and it can be nurtured and made visible.
- By rehearsing, you have time to get comfortable with the drill of speaking in public. You learn by doing.
- As you are able to take ownership of your performance, confidence will automatically start to kick in.
- Never compare your presenting skills with someone else's. EVER.
- Self-talk plays a profound role in sports, in presenting and in life. What's yours saying to you?

Chapter 4: The Spoken Word and How to Sound Real

"An identical spoken and written language would be practically intolerable; if we spoke as we write, we should find no one to listen; and if we wrote as we speak, we should find no one to read." T.S. Eliot

Introduction

How a speaker bridges the two types of language to which Eliot refers determines who will bore an audience and who will hook and hold them.

Think of all the canned elevator pitches you've heard. They sound stilted because they're not written with natural speech in mind. You can hear the keyboard as people rattle their way through pitches that are always too long and impossible to follow.

This is where we learn to focus our knowledge, energy, and time on getting excellent performance results by writing the script that will ring true to an audience.

All Politics Is Local

My next speaker was willing to get rid of the washed-out phrases and clichéd vocabulary in his line of work, which is politics. He was open to taking direction and advice that differed from the industry standard. He went on to win his election based on who he *really* was and how he normally spoke.

We first met at the Department of Motor Vehicles, of all places, after I asked to see the manager to complain about a worker. Clive was that manager, and he handled the situation beautifully. It turned out to be a temporary position for him, a political favor. He said he planned to run for office himself within the next six months.

He'd been a member of the Young Republicans in the mid-1960s and was fascinated by the game. For decades, he'd been a regular behind-the-scenes player on other's elections but had only once run for office himself. He lost that race. He was crushed. I was transfixed.

As he told me the story, there was something so genuine and appealing about Clive that I gave him my card, figuring that the same principles of good speaking should apply to being on the stump. Though I'd never coached a politician and have never been drawn to politics, he hired me anyway, and I joined his team. He planned to run for an office in his hometown.

At our first meeting, Clive asked, "Are you a Republican, a Democrat, or a hired gun?" I laughed, looked him in the eye, and said, "Just a hired gun. My job is to get you elected." Then I asked him about his experience giving speeches, and it was...completely lacking.

We met a couple of times after that for coffee, talking about how he might position himself as a candidate.

From my perspective, what he had going for him were his sincerity and an exhaustive knowledge of local government. What I had was the benefit of zero experience with politics, which meant that I didn't know the boilerplate speech lingo that everyone else uses, and couldn't be distracted by it.

We focused on Clive's upbringing, his life-long belief in the GOP, and his history of watching everything from the sidelines. How would all of this shape and influence his new "voice?" I nixed his campaign manager's opening lines: "My fellow Americans, I stand before you today, a man who has decided to run for office in this great state of New Jersey." That was the voice of the political speech writer, but not Clive.

The phrasing wasn't a good fit for him; he didn't normally talk like that. We ended up co-writing a script much more like his natural speech that included his father's advice to "stay out of politics...it's a rotten business!" That line got a good laugh every time. Clive was straightforward, transparent, and charming.

He was fun to work with because he enjoyed himself and loved everything involved in running for office, from working the train platforms at 5 am greeting crabby commuters to speaking at endless dinners on the rubber chicken circuit. His message connected well with his constituents in a genuine way that was palpable. He was, undeniably, a glow worm. He was voted into office.

It was the culmination of a dream twenty-five years in the making and he did it. Clive had focus and his goal was crystalline for him, so *all* his actions were naturally oriented toward achieving it. Nothing else mattered as much to him, so he was able to shrug off set-backs quickly.

From the Roots

N ow I'll tell you about Rosa and her challenges to communicating clearly and staying true to herself. She worked in a light-filled office facing Rockefeller Plaza. She was a financial analyst in the energy sector, and like all of her colleagues, she was whip-smart, competitive, and industrious.

Rosa had something extra, though. This quality let her stick with her convictions at a time when everyone around her on Wall Street were losing theirs: Rosa consistently refused to invest in Enron. Jeff Skilling himself called to bully her when she kept turning his people away. She still said no. This prudence saved her clients millions of dollars.

I came to coach her for a debriefing she was going to present to her portfolio's board of advisors. We would write and rehearse her Enron success story, one of very few in existence. We had three weeks for prep, and then she would fly to Los Angeles where she would give her talk four times over two days of meetings.

Good content can be enhanced by the perfect story. For Rosa, the way she analyzed the information (which everyone else had) turns out to have been guided by her father, a highly respected homicide detective in Queens.

His advice to Rosa had always been (both in general and especially in business) to keep asking questions until she was satisfied that she knew what happened. If she couldn't figure it out, then she stayed on it until she got her questions answered.

His counsel immediately came into play when she tried to read Enron's financial reports and found them incomprehensible. Of course, their management wrote them that way, calculating that few analysts would bother to examine them closely and that the popularity of the stock would be enough to sell it. Rosa, it turns out, was listening to her father, not Wall Street, and that's where the real story was.

However, when it came time to write the script, she wanted to take a boilerplate, corporate-speak approach and not use her real voice, which is quick-witted and slightly irreverent. I asked her why she wanted to hide behind a tone that wasn't who she was, and after a while she said, "I'm not comfortable in front of these people." Hmmm.

I asked to see photos and bios of everyone who would be in her audience, and as we looked at them together, my immediate comment was how Ivy League and WASP-y they all looked.

And *that's* when we both saw the reason for Rosa's resistance. The daughter of the detective keenly felt the difference between her background and theirs, which caused her to feel "less than" by comparison, just as Asher thought of himself as less than Darius on the television talk show. These were the feelings impeding her ability to own her message.

Starting from the outside in, we decided to style her as "one of them." We went with a pastel sweater twin-set, double strand of pearls, and black headband, and voila! She now had a costume that allowed her to blend in visually and helped her get into her role.

In her report, rather than masking her heritage, she paid homage to her father by mentioning his formula for success and emphasized that it was precisely *because* of her background that she cracked a code that no one else did.

Both external and internal choices allowed her to create a fresh relationship with herself and her upcoming audiences. In rehearsal, she found a new side of herself, one that was strong, compelling, and in command when speaking in front of people she'd previously been intimidated by. Now, Rosa was ready for show time.

In Los Angeles, she delivered her speech four times to different audiences. She called, very excited, to tell me that three times they *applauded* at the end of her presentation. This is something she assured me *never* happens – and yet, it did. She was blown away by this, but I wasn't a bit surprised.

So in spite of a mountain of empirical proof that she knew her stuff, it was Rosa's feelings that had to be managed and adjusted. It's true for formal presenting, but it also comes up every day in the routine and the mundane. The next chapter shows you how to make the most of those times.

Key points from Chapter 4:

- Writing for the spoken word is different than writing for the written word, so adjust your style accordingly.
- Don't be afraid to dream big for your speaking skills; you could win your next election.

- Don't allow yourself to be pressured into being someone you're not.
- Address any internal discomfort you might be having, so you can manage it immediately.
- Styling yourself for the event can make it easier to slip into your "role."
- Believe in yourself, and stay open to applause.

Chapter 5: Rehearsing

"You win, not by chance, but by preparation." Roger Maris

Introduction

Y ou'll have noticed by now that each speaker's story involves rehearsing once the script is nailed down. Think of rehearsing as your incubator time, where you and your message develop and grow into one.

Just in case you may think that rehearsing is unnecessary, let me tell you about Dannie.

The Bully

M y youngest client to date was nine years old when we worked together. I don't normally coach children, but her mother was a friend, and the matter was urgent: her daughter Dannie was being bullied at school.

When they first came to me, I listened to the story and wondered how to proceed, but the answer was soon as clear as the problem. Here was a young, African American girl who was bright and sweet but baffled as to why she was being singled out for abuse. The bully was making racist comments when no one else was around.

I told Dannie I was sorry she had to deal with this business at her age but that what she was about to learn would be a skill she'd always have.

We practiced our news for the bully, which was the plain truth: "Where I come from, there is zero tolerance for bullying, so either you tell the teacher what you've said to me, or I will. It's your choice." We included some arm movements for special effect, rehearsing until she had them down. They were sweeping gestures, meant to expand Dannie's energy outward (because she's so tiny). I drilled her as hard as I drilled Asher, and she was able to come across as firm and fearless. She was ready for show time.

Now armed and prepared, Dannie sought out her tormentor. The bully, meanwhile, sensing that Dannie's energy had made an about-face, avoided her. Inevitably, there came a showdown. At the bus stop, Dannie spotted the girl, took her aside, and delivered her message. She did it just as she had rehearsed it, and said she felt calm and clear when it was over.

The bully stayed out of school for the next three days! When she finally returned, she cheerfully announced that she wanted to be Dannie's friend; Dannie immediately declined the offer. Dannie had learned an important lesson about sticking up for herself, and now she was ready to move on. Today, she's a happy, well-adjusted kid, and her mom says she has more confidence than ever.

The key to this success was that we rehearsed rehearsed rehearsed. She was effective because she was ready—and she was ready because we practiced.

The legendary basketball coach John Wooden said, "The importance of repetition until automaticity cannot be overstated. Repetition is the key to learning." Wooden drilled his players to stay in the moment and focus on the game, not the outcome. He was able to get great results because they were well prepared (rehearsed) for each game. (Remember that the French word for rehearsal *is répétition*!)

Tip #1: Listen to the Sound

W hen you begin to rehearse, do so in private, so you can try on words and see how they affect you without feeling self-conscious. Move around as you speak. Then once you feel the flow of your ideas and are confident that things make sense to you out loud, start recording yourself. (All smart phones have audio and video recording apps for things like this.) Having said that, it's also important not to rush to record yourself, as well as not to delay it.

Take it nice and easy, and don't try to give a finished performance. Simply get a sense of how it feels to be "on."

Are you tripping over the same phrase each time you read it? Smooth it out so you can voice it comfortably. Swap any words you have trouble pronouncing for something easier, because if you're struggling with them in private, it will only get worse in public.

Do you sound rushed? All spoken language has its own rhythm, with some points needing more time than others to get their meaning across. Play with your pacing to learn where you want to take time to emphasize a point and where you can move along more quickly.

Take your time while you learn your speech so that can find nuance and coloring that would otherwise be lost if you just whipped through it without actually feeling it.

Tip #2: See What You're Saying

Visualize what you're talking about. For example, let's say my script has this line: "Teddy Kennedy said that Cape Cod is one of the most beautiful places on earth" (actual words of his).

While I'm saying those words, my mind visualizes a real beach at the Cape. I see bright sun on the water, I see sparkle and flash. Waves are swelling high, and there's chop in the water and gulls on the wing, shrieking who knows what to each other. In an instant, I am inside the words, through the image.

Visualizing parts of your script enriches the spoken word because the brain is more deeply connecting with those words as images. In some of my own scripts, I've included photos in the page margins to help me voice the feeling I'm going for. I'll also use colors on the page to suggest different moods or vocal tones.

"Visualizing" also means easily seeing what's on the page. If I'm reading my script, I'll make sure there are no "widows and orphans" on any of the pages to cause a pause in my delivery where I don't want one.

I'll also go up to a larger font (as we did with my husband John). This makes it easier to find my place at a glance, which supports me during my delivery. I've seen speakers get into trouble because they're not able to look from their script to their audience and back to the script. Rehearsing will smooth this out. You'll learn how to read, feel, and speak at the same time.

Tip #3: Looking Ahead to Looking Out

If you want to deliver in a more free-form style, then take the script you've fleshed out and create bullet points. Your brain has done the work of thinking it through, so highlight the major words and phrases that have meaning for you and make those your touchstones. I also suggest doing your bullet points only *after* you have gone through the process and discipline of writing out your speech.

I strongly advise against deciding what points are most important while standing in front of an audience because of the risk of rambling on and thus coming across as not being knowledgeable (even when you are). You also run the risk of not being able to track what you've already said and what still needs to be covered.

I've had clients tell me that they don't want to use cue cards or scripts because they think these are signs of being a weak speaker.

This strikes me as a false measure of someone's skills; I don't care what a speaker has to do to hook my interest and keep it. That's not my concern; I only want to be taken care of when I commit myself to being in an audience. After all, it's my time and energy, and I'm just there for a positive experience, not to fault someone for using props.

Tip #4: Approximate your delivery styling in your run-throughs

After you feel sure you know what you're saying and feel comfortable with how you're saying it, you should then rehearse in the clothes that you will be wearing for your actual event.

For example, if I decide that I'm going to wear a higher heel for my speech because I feel empowered by them, I should wear the actual shoes, or an approximation, which lets me practice with the energy of coming from strength. Also, if I'm going to deliver my speech standing up, then I have to rehearse standing up, which will also tell me if my empowerment shoes are actually comfortable enough to wear.

If you're wearing a suit and tie for your speech, rehearse in a jacket. You don't want an ill-fitting suit or sloppy tie distracting you from the message you've worked so diligently to create.

This is your "dress rehearsal" and it's called that precisely for this reason! (For more on style and wardrobe, see the next chapter.)

Tip #5: Q and A

I ask my speakers to list every possible question they think *might* be raised and then have them practice the answers until they are fluent and concise. A good Q & A can be a pivotal moment in your success because if you can connect with an audience member, others will want to participate, too. That's when the magic of live events can spark up, because everyone is focusing on the same thing at the same time in the same space. I like to describe a dynamic back-and-forth between speaker and audience as "porous."

On the other hand, not all questions may be genuine, especially if someone in the audience wants to grab the spotlight away from you and on to them. My advice for handling a question like this is to politely and firmly halt them in their tracks, then make a calm but unwavering suggestion to continue the matter in private. If they persist, you must persist. As the presenter, you're the one who controls the focus and the flow as well as the only one authorized to keep order.

Let's say you don't have a ready answer for a question. This is when you say, "I'll get back to you on that." There is no shame in saying that you don't have an answer, only in pretending that you do when you don't.

Tip #6: Managing Expectations

T his step of your prep has to do with how you anticipate feeling before, during, and after you present.

By thinking ahead to show time, for example, you have to factor in your adrenaline rush and how the following symptoms might affect you.

- Racing heart and shallow breathing
- Sweating
- Shaking in voice, hands, feet, knees, and body parts you didn't know you had
- Pitch of the voice goes up
- Entire body has a sense of RED ALERT

These signs are normal and do not signal impending doom. Your rehearsal allows you to manage this before it happens. Acknowledge that you'll be having physical changes in your body.

This is one fix you'll definitely benefit from, what the Army calls "Tactical Breathing," also known as yoga breathing. Take a deep inhalation from the diaphragm (under your ribs and lower than chest) on a slow count of five. Now hold that deep breath for a count of five, then release it on a count of five. Repeat as needed until you feel settled and grounded in your body and clear in your mind.

As you get your breathing under control, bring in your mantra so that your brain lifts you up immediately into the mental realm of positive possibility. The mantra will re-route the energy of an adrenaline rush into empowered inspiration.

Think of it not as stage *fright* but as stage *energy*, and you will find that it feels wonderful.

__Key Points of Chapter 5:__

- Don't let anyone bully you. Ever. Tell them why you don't accept their words.
- Practice makes perfect, or "repetition is the key to learning."
- Don't push yourself to come up with an instant "performance." Begin in private and take your time.
- Take advantage of simple rehearsal tools on your smart phone, such as the timer and voice notes.
- Let yourself discover the organic rhythm of your piece.
- Visualize what you're talking about a split second before you say the words.
- Use images and colors in your script/speaker notes.

Chapter 6: Style and Substance

"Fashion is about dressing according to what's fashionable. Style is more about being yourself." Oscar de la Renta

Introduction

We learn here how to dress and prep for show time, just as in the theater, where costumes and styling are treated as part of the story line. We also learn how to eat like an athlete on game day.

Styling

When you're a presenter for a formal event, you'll want to style yourself with a bit of flair. The first thing people will notice is the color of your clothing, so for show time, I advise wearing "power colors," including touches of red, orange, ruby, sapphire, purple, and others in that palette. (Please note that I say *touches*. Be sure not to do head-to-toe bright cherry, but a shirt, shoes, or a tie in that color can make a vibrant first impression, especially if your audience, as is often the case, is dressed in the ubiquitous head-to-toe business black, gray, or blue.)

Ensure that what you wear fits you well. Charles, one of my speakers, was giving an important keynote speech on water conservation in southern California, so a tux had been rented for him and alterations made.

But when he tried it on at the tailor's, he found himself swimming in it and threatened not to go onstage wearing it. The tux was quickly returned for more work, resulting in a much better fit. Charles was able to go on stage feeling pulled-together, which fed his confidence. Then he got a standing ovation. Did he get it because of his tux? No, but the tux did not get in his way. It supported him onstage, and that's why he succeeded.

Hairstyling for men can be as simple as a good haircut and beard trim. For women, the haircut should work well for business, be age-appropriate, and be colored or treated well.

For hair and make-up, Glamsquad.com is a fantastic app-based beauty service for women living in New York, L.A. and Miami. Their expert teams come to your house and can do your hair, makeup, manicure, and pedicure. All these treatments create a professional and positive difference in your energy, especially when it's showtime!

Shoes need to be in good shape and polished, and above all, comfortable and supportive. Women will have to make a decision about heels or not, but for me, when presenting, I don't want to depend on a teeny piece of a high heel to physically connect me to the earth and steady me for my presentation. Rather, I'll wear a well-made ankle boot that empowers me as it stabilizes me.

Like everything else in this list, jewelry should complement rather than dominate. I've seen some stunning jewels at networking events, client meetings, and conventions, but it's always best not to overdo it and keep it simple.

For more casual events, the styling "rules" are less strict. If you choose jeans, make sure they flatter you. I'm a big fan of NYDJ for this reason. (NYDJ stands for "Not Your Daughter's Jeans.") The length should be right; have a professional do any alterations. Pockets stuffed with too many things can ruin the line of the garment.

Jackets, shirts, blouses, tee shirts, and so on should fit you well and be in good shape.

And last, but not least, whether the event is formal or not, make sure to give yourself a once-over (teeth, hair, outfit) before you leave, and again when you arrive. When I present, I have a kit with a lint roller, toothbrush, floss, neutral powder, mirror, safety pins, cough drops, lip balm, and Kleenex. You have to act as your own "crew" because once you start, no one is going to interrupt you to let you know you have kale in your teeth!

When you look smart in the right outfit, it all feeds into a strong sense of confidence for the job at hand and presents you as the authority that you are. As Shakespeare tells us "All the world's a stage." Be ready to go on looking the part you want to play.

Food

I f you are what you eat, then you want to match the food to the event. You never want to present on either a full or an empty stomach. Smart food choices include fresh vegetables and fruits, nuts, whole grains, lean proteins, nothing fried, and minimal sugar. Instead of pizza and fast-foods, go for salads, wraps, and soups.

Eat a balanced breakfast on presenting day, even if you're not slated to speak until much later, and be sure to have enough snacks during the day to keep your blood sugar even. Oatmeal is a good choice because it's a slow-burning carbohydrate, as is a breakfast burrito or granola with fruit.

Eggs are fine but avoid cheese, milk, yogurt, chocolate, and anything with milk or cream, which can cause "sticky mouth" and affect your diction. This becomes especially noticeable when you're speaking into a microphone. Keep sipping water and brush your teeth.

Avoid bagels because of their high glycemic load and also sugary muffins, shakes, or pastry. Because they cause your blood sugar levels to spike, they can leave you feeling fatigued and shaky.

Don't eat anything immediately before you speak because it starts up your saliva production. So stay hydrated before, during, and after. Un-carbonated water either cool or at room temperature, is the speaker's beverage of choice. Don't ever drink alcohol until *after* your presentation, when you're raising a glass to toast yourself for a job well done. Do limit or avoid caffeine on presenting day as it can amplify your adrenaline and effect your ability to keep calm and focused. Try an herbal tea instead.

Meals are also a significant part of a career, which means that etiquette matters. Walt Bettinger, the CEO of Charles Schwab, invites prospective hires to join him for breakfast and then secretly instructs the kitchen to mess up their order. This lets him get a close look at how they handle pressure as well as their cutlery. Be aware of the conventions.

- If you're seated at a table for any meal, the first thing to do is put your napkin in your lap. It's all right to put your elbows on the table if nothing has yet been served or if everything has been cleared away. Otherwise, they stay tucked in at your sides.
- Properly placed cutlery works from the outside in. So a salad fork will be to the left of the entrée fork. If in doubt, just start at the outer perimeter and work your way in. Never put an in-use utensil on the table, or half-on the plate and half-on the table. It stays on the plate.
- Don't slurp anything, ever, except an oyster.
- If you're at an event serving wine in a wine glass, hold it by the stem or the base. The theory is that cupping the main part of the glass will affect the temperature of the wine. If you're drinking wine out of a plastic cup, you have nothing to worry about.
- Avoid soup unless it's clam chowder on the beach.
- Turn your phone off before the meal and leave it off until it's over.
- If you have to blow your nose, leave the table.
- Don't slouch down to meet your fork, bring it up to you.
- Never scrape your leftovers onto another plate at the table.
- Don't groom yourself at the table.
- Hold your utensils properly.

The Last Supper

This next story didn't happen to me, but I heard it from the woman who was there. May it serve as a cautionary tale.

It concerns a corporate shoot for American Express, which is when director, producers, camera crews, hair and makeup, lighting, and so on, all meet either in a television studio or onsite at a location. They're usually working with execs (meaning they are not actors and usually uncomfortable on/camera) and shoots can be long and tedious. A good director on the set makes all the difference in everyone's day.

That day, the script was an unusually complicated one. The director was a freelancer, and it was a big chance for him. If he did well, he'd have a shot at joining the regular stable of directors on the AMEX staff.

Well, the guy was on fire. He handled the complexities of the day in a professional and poised manner. He coaxed better performances from the executives than anyone had been able to. AMEX was happy, and he was thrilled.

When the shoot wrapped, the execs wanted to take everyone to dinner. They headed over to the popular French restaurant Balthazar and proceeded to have a fantastic time. They started with wine, talked the day over, marveled at how well the shoot went, and had a delicious dinner.

The director feels expansive and successful, so when the bill comes, he picks it up. Everyone has coffee and when they're all set to go, he pulls his Master Card out of his wallet and puts it on the table. All eyes go to the card, and then back to the director. He never worked for them again.

Key points from Chapter 6:

- Before you can open your mouth, your styling is already sending out a message-do you know what yours is saying about you?
- The fit and color of your wardrobe affect your energy as well as the first impression you make.
- Professional styling for big events is great not only for your appearance, but also your morale.
- Your shoes are where you are connected to the earth.
- Eat a high-protein breakfast, skip/cut back on caffeine, and sip lots of water on presentation day.
- Never drink alcohol to manage your performance nerves as it will affect your delivery and send the wrong message.
- Don't eat just before presenting. A slightly empty stomach is ideal.
- Table etiquette matters and you could be judged by it, so it pays to brush up on it. "Ignorance of the law is no excuse."
- Brand awareness and sensitivity is of huge importance to business owners.

Chapter 7: The Importance of Networking

"Networking is an essential part of building wealth." Armstrong Williams

Introduction

O ften, the informal and less structured interactions at events can have the biggest benefits. Being articulate in small-group conversations, talking "shop" with peers–on the golf course, at the local coffee shop–these help you be seen as an industry participant even more than that fantastic speech you just delivered twenty minutes ago. As Ben Jonson put it so eloquently in 1619, "Language most shows a man; speak, that I may see thee!" Don't be shy about speaking up for yourself, your values, and your beliefs.

Networking Tips

T here are so many ways to network these days, and you can't get to all of them. You need a strategy that will put you in close proximity to people who are good for you to meet.

Go with a clear intention: "I'm going to introduce myself to the first person I see." Or decide that you'll stay for exactly one hour or stay until you've had three productive conversations. Make your intentions easy to remember and easy to enact.

Acoustics matter. If the sound in the venue is too loud for regular conversation to develop, it's a waste of time. You can't be yourself or get to know anyone else if you have to yell to be heard. I now avoid certain places in New York City because of this.

Then, once you arrive in a low-key atmosphere where the acoustics are good, conversation starters are easy-peasy. Some examples:

- Do you know anyone here?
- I love your necklace.
- Do you work near here?
- Where did you get your shoes?
- Where's the bar?
- Are they serving food?
- Do you have a card?
- Did you pick that tie out, or did someone else?
- Anything that comes to mind. It doesn't need to be savvy, just enough to get the ball rolling.

Don't attach yourself to one person, and don't let anyone do that to you, since it defeats the point of meeting new people and making fresh contacts. Personally, I excuse myself if I find I've been more than ten minutes in one spot. And I don't offer "I'll be back" or "I have to make a call" but simply "I've enjoyed meeting you."

Remember that your goal is to bring back cards or other promotional pieces of potential business contacts. These are your hunting trophies, and what you do with them matters.

When you're handed a card, take time to look at it; don't pocket it without really seeing it. Take a few notes on it, which will help you recall the conversation you have with its owner. Do this in the moment, instead of thinking you'll remember later (you won't).

The following day, spread them out. Keep those that seem like a good fit for your business. The goal is to develop relationships that are enjoyable and genuine, and those take time and energy. Just because someone gives you a card doesn't mean you should keep it.

Look up the websites on the cards you keep. (I've been surprised more than once to find a card with a non-existent website.) If I like the website, I'll check their social media presence. Typically, most of my contacts are on LinkedIn, so I'll send an invitation to connect, but I'll make sure to personalize the invitation...to take an extra few minutes to say something meaningful about them and their professional interests and profile.

From there, I'll write to them to ask permission to put them on my e-list. Once there, I can maintain contact with them and deepen the connection over time. The one big mistake that a lot of people make at networking events is to ask for something too soon.

If you've just met a man, you don't ask him what kind of entrée he'd like to serve at your wedding. When you meet someone at an event, don't immediately ask for a favor...i.e. could you introduce me to so-and-so, will you like me on FB, may I send you my resume etc.

It's a turn-off, so don't do it.

__Key points from Chapter 7__

- Casual events can yield big results, so always bring your A game!
- Acoustics matter. If you can't converse, you can't communicate.
- Networking is like a sport, so play strategically.
- Don't ask for favors right away.
- Take notes on business cards, or else you'll never make sense of them later.
- You don't have to come up with a brilliant opening line, just enough to get the ball rolling.

Chapter 8: Blaze Away

"Be a light unto yourself." Buddha Shakyamuni

This is what you need to know when you're ready to start working on your own show.

We began this book with Isaac and the International Rescue Committee. With Dina, another person I met through the IRC, I close it.

She was a newly widowed woman, in her early 30s, with toddlers aged two and four.

Terrorists in Baghdad had killed her beloved husband, and she was forced to flee Iraq with her children and mother in a harrowing night-time escape. They survived in refugee camps for a few years, and I met her four months after she arrived in the United States. Once again, I would be coaching a first-time speaker for a high-stakes black-tie event.

Her ability to connect with an audience would be a chance to show everyone proof of the humanity and dignity that their donations made possible. Though we didn't discuss this, we both knew that literally lives were at stake and depending on her being clear about had happened to her.

Like Isaac, she'd never given a speech, not in English or Arabic. In her life, women didn't speak in public often, if ever. She'd been well educated and grew up in a house full of books and lively intellectual conversation, but her father and brothers were the public face of the family.

What we had in our favor was that her English was excellent—she'd been an interpreter for the US military—and she was fearless enough to give her account of the war in Iraq.

We talked about what happened in Baghdad – a very, very tough conversation. We distilled her story down to five minutes (that was the hardest part) and co-wrote the script. We were permitted to use two slides for added dramatic value.

We chose one that was a stunning sunset photo of the pre-war Baghdad skyline, and the other was of Dina and her husband smiling sweetly at the camera.

She knew she had this one chance to say her piece and that she had to make the most of it, no matter what. If she forgot a line or felt too emotional, she would still have to push through. We rehearsed right up until she had to go onstage; then once again, the esteemed Tom Brokaw introduced her, and she was on.

She stepped into the spotlight and became mesmerizing and magnificent as she gave her searing testimony of living with terrorism and the grace of surviving. People were moved to tears and then to cheers when she finished. The minute she stepped off-stage, people surrounded her, wanting to meet her and congratulate her. The night was a major success on all levels; the emotions she stirred in the audience would eventually contribute to the rescue of many more families and lives. But most importantly for Dina, she had been able to "share her being" with an audience of strangers, and when she came off-stage, she was beaming just as she had been in that picture with her husband.

A few weeks later, she called to say that giving the speech had changed how she sees herself. She found herself standing up straight instead of assuming her protective slouch with arms crossed in front of her. She went on to tell me she'd been speaking up more and expressing her opinions often. Knowing she was setting a confident example for herself, her children, and her mother was clearly agreeing with her.

Like all of the others in this book, Dina has gone on to be a guest speaker at other events. Derek ran two workshops and gave a keynote speech at the Kennedy Center. Clive just called to arrange a few rehearsals for a bill he's going to present in Trenton, his state's capital. After that, he's planning on running for higher office. Rosa left her job and opened her own hedge fund. She has shown herself to be engaging, social, and vocal, thereby attracting clients who are a perfect fit for her.

My husband John eulogized his father a few years ago. We got to work together, once again, and in two weeks we had everything ready.

At the church, John stepped into place and spoke, and as he did, he was so clearly in the spirit of the moment that we were all one with him.

When he concluded, his father's casket was slowly wheeled towards the back of the church, and as the casket passed by the pews, the whole congregation gave the procession a standing ovation!

The owner of the funeral parlor said to me in a stunned voice, "In thirty-five years, that has never happened." All I could say was "My father-in-law was a great guy" because he really was.

These are the times in our lives when it's invaluable to be able to verbalize our deepest, dearest beliefs, and for my husband, this was definitely one of them. Imagining that in your life, what would you choose to speak out about, and what would that mean for your business, your family and friends, your life?

Key points of Chapter 8:

* Lack of presenting experience doesn't stop some people from being able to deliver well, while lack of information about how to prepare is the real barrier, easily removed.
* Miracles can and do happen...I've seen several.
* Many places welcome good content, and some will pay you for it.
* Experience builds confidence.
* Once you can present from the stage, it's easy to adapt for on/camera and podcasts.

Au Revoir

"Use your powers only for good."

How to Take Your Show On the Road

When you're almost ready to put yourself in front of the public, you'll start your marketing process. This entails putting together some promotional material about your presentation. Write two to three paragraphs and include some photos, testimonials if you have them, and video clips. Be clear about your topic, how long it is, and, when you have it, feedback from people.

Many places need good content, and each community will have its own resources for outlets. Libraries are perfect. They not only need material for adult learning programs, they can also tell you whom else you might approach. The same goes for community centers and chambers of commerce. Meet Ups are also ideal proving grounds.

Book stores often host events, and churches, temples, and mosques do as well. In fact, any business, organization, or club related to your topic could be a potential venue for you.

Each time that you get out there is another notch in your belt. It gives you that much more information and experience. Your speaking skills will grow, develop, and change over time.

Once you can deliver to a live audience and you have a feel for it, and have some events under your belt, you can adapt it for video and record it. Having this as a marketing tool lets you post it on-line and promote yourself to entirely new communities and galaxies.

The conversations, surveys, and research that comprise this book were as illuminating as they were inspiring. They confirm what I've long known: that everyone has what it takes to do an excellent job of presenting ideas that really matter and need to be heard.

If you'd like to talk with me about your struggle with public speaking, shoot me an email at Katie@onspeakingterms. com If you'd like a phone call, include your number.